Friend IS FOREVER

A HELEN EXLEY
GIFTBOOK

EXLEY

*With a friend at your
side no road
seems too long.*

JAPANESE PROVERB

*Friendship improves
happiness, and abates
misery, by doubling our
joy, and dividing
our grief.*

JOSEPH ADDISON

*We have been
friends together;
in sunshine
and in shade.*

CAROLINE NORTON

One's friends are that part of the human race with which one can be human.

GEORGE SANTAYANA

May friendship like wine, improve as time advances. And may we always have old wine, old friends, and young cares.

TRADITIONAL

A friend hears the song in my heart and sings it to me when my memory fails.

FROM "PIONEER GIRLS
LEADERS' HANDBOOK"

That is the best – to laugh with someone because you both think the same things are funny.

GLORIA VANDERBILT

The proper office of a friend is to side with you when you are in the wrong. Nearly anybody will side with you when you are in the right.

MARK TWAIN

*Best friend,
my well-spring
in the wilderness.*

GEORGE ELIOT
(MARY ANN EVANS)

No one can

develop freely in

this world and find

a full life without

feeling understood

by at least one

person.

PAUL TOURNIER

*Hold a true friend
with both your hands.*

NIGERIAN PROVERB

*[Friends] stand there
as a solid and
impregnable bulwark
against all the evils
of life.*

SYDNEY SMITH

The test of friendship
is assistance
in adversity, and that,
too, unconditional
assistance.

MAHATMA GANDHI

Silences make the real conversations between friends. Not the saying but the never needing to say is what counts.

MARGARET LEE RUNBECK

Of all the things which wisdom provides to make life entirely happy, much the greatest is the possession of friendship.

EPICURUS

A mile walked with a friend contains only a hundred steps.

RUSSIAN PROVERB

*True friends
are those
seeking solitude
together.*

ABEL BONNARD

A friend, by a phone call, a popping-in, a chance meeting, a small unexpected surprise, puts a little jam on the day's bread and butter.

J . R . C .

Friendship is the only cement that will ever hold the world together.

WOODROW WILSON

There is nothing final between friends.

WILLIAM BRYAN

*Knowing you are
somewhere –
near or far – means
I'm never, never
totally alone.*

MARION C. GARRETTY

*In
prosperity
our friends
know us;
In adversity
we know
our friends.*

J.M. BARRIE

In a thousand wuys [my friends] have turned my limitations into beautiful privileges, and enabled me to walk serene and happy in the shadow cast by my deprivation.

HELEN KELLER

When you meet a
man, you judge him
by his clothes;
When you leave,
you judge him by
his heart.

RUSSIAN PROVERB

Friendships that have stood the test of time and change are surely best.

JOSEPH PARRY

We need friendship
all the time, just as
much as we need the
proverbial prime
necessities of life,
fire and water.

CICERO

A friend is a person with whom I may be sincere. Before him I may think aloud.

RALPH WALDO EMERSON

The language of friendship is not words but meanings.

HENRY DAVID THOREAU

So long as we are loved by others, we are indispensable; and no man is useless while he has a friend.

ROBERT LOUIS STEVENSON

Nothing
can
come
between
true
friends.

EURIPIDES

$\mathcal{F}$riends do
not live in
harmony merely,
as some say,
but in melody.

HENRY DAVID THOREAU

*Each friend represents
a world in us,
a world possibly not
born until they arrive,
and it is only by this
meeting that a new
world is born.*

ANAÏS NIN

*We do not mind
our not arriving
anywhere nearly so
much as our not
having any company
on the way.*

FRANK MOORE COLBY

Wherever you are it is your own friends who make your world.

WILLIAM JAMES

*Friendships link
and loop and interweave
until they mesh the world.*

PAM BROWN

*In my friend,
I find a
second self.*

ISABEL NORTON

A friend knows how

to allow for mere

quantity in your talk,

and only replies

to the quality....

WILLIAM DEAN HOWELLS

Seeing a good friend is like going home, or like tasting Mother's cooking. I feel secure, and need not protect myself. "Here," I say, "it is safe, for I am loved."

ARNOLD R. BEISSER

As long as there is a
post and the telephone is
not cut off, so long as we
have things to tell and
joys and anxieties to share –
we will be friends.

MARION C. GARRETTY

Friendship multiplies the good of life and divides the evil. 'Tis the sole remedy against misfortune, the very ventilation of the soul.

BALTASAR GRACIAN

*What is
a friend?
A single soul
dwelling in
two bodies.*

ARISTOTLE

*There's nothing
worth the wear
of winning,
but laughter and
the love of friends.*

HILAIRE BELLOC

... *friendship, the ease of it,
it is not something to be
taken lightly – nor for
granted. Because, after
breathing and eating and
sleeping, friendships are
essential to our survival.*

ADELAIDE BRY

When friendship once

is rooted fast

It is a plant

no storm can blast.

FROM A 19TH-CENTURY
CALLING CARD

$\mathcal{W}$e are not primarily put
on the earth to see through
one another, but to see one
another through.

PETER DE VRIES

Trouble is a sieve
through which we
sift our acquaintances.
Those too big to
pass through are
our friends.

ARLENE FRANCIS

*When a
friend asks
there is
no tomorrow.*

GEORGE HERBERT

I trust that even when I'm out of sight I'm not out of mind. Silences and distances are woven into the texture of every true friendship.

ROBERTA ISRAELOFF

Friends, companions,
lovers, are those
who treat us in terms
of our unlimited worth
to ourselves.

HENRY ALONZO MYERS

[Friends] are closest to us who best understand what life means to us, who feel for us as we feel for ourselves, who are bound to us in triumph and disaster, who break the spell of our loneliness.

HENRY ALONZO MYERS

A friend is the one
who comes in when
the whole world has
gone out.

ALBAN GOODIER

*If you accompany
a friend, there is
no detour too far.*

LEO TOLSTOY

Grief can take care of itself, but to get the full value of a joy you must have somebody to divide it with.

MARK TWAIN

The most I can
do for my friend
is simply to be
his friend.

HENRY DAVID THOREAU

True friendship comes

when silence between

two people is

comfortable.

DAVE TYSON GENTRY

What do we live for, if it is not to make life less difficult for each other?

GEORGE ELIOT
(MARY ANN EVANS)

Friendship is unnecessary, like philosopy, like art... It has no survival value; rather it is one of those things that give value to survival.

C. S. LEWIS

*The bird a nest,
the spider a web,
man friendship.*

WILLIAM BLAKE

*Happiness
seems made
to be shared.*

JEAN RACINE

*Friendship's
the wine
of life.*

EDWARD YOUNG

Friendship without self-interest is one of the rare and beautiful things of life.

JAMES BYRNES

*Wishing to be friends
is quick work,
but friendship is a
slow-ripening fruit.*

ARISTOTLE

*Friendship
is a
sheltering
tree.*

SAMUEL TAYLOR COLERIDGE

Your friend is the man who knows all about you, and still likes you.

ELBERT HUBBARD

Friendship, a dear balm...
A smile among dark frowns: a beloved light:
A solitude, a refuge, a delight.

PERCY BYSSHE SHELLEY

One can do

without people,

but one has

need of a friend.

CHINESE PROVERB

*Cooperation
is spelled
with two
letters: we.*

G.M. VERITY

It is one of the
blessings of old
friends that you
can afford to be
stupid with them.

RALPH WALDO EMERSON

I always felt that the great high privilege, relief and comfort of friendship was that one had to explain nothing.

KATHERINE MANSFIELD

Friend derives from a word meaning "free". A friend is someone who allows us the space and freedom to be.

DEBBIE ALICEN

My friend is one who likes me for what I am.

HENRY DAVID THOREAU

To have even one
good friend is to
keep the darkness
at bay.

PAM BROWN

Trouble shared is
trouble halved.

DOROTHY SAYERS

... True Blue Friends...

make you feel good

and warm; they are

automatically on the

same wavelength.

ADELAIDE BRY

*Don't walk in front of
me, I may not follow.
Don't walk behind me, I
may not lead.
Walk beside me, and just
be my friend.*

AUTHOR UNKNOWN

For whoever knows how to return a kindness he has received must be a friend above all price.

SOPHOCLES

When a person that one loves is in the world and alive and well... then to miss them is only a new flavour, a salt sharpness in experience.

WINIFRED HOLTBY

What is a friend?
I will tell you.
It is a person with
whom you dare to
be yourself.

FRANK CRANE

*O*ld friends are
best. King James
used to call for
his old shoes;
they were easiest
for his feet.

JOHN SELDON

*Because I got you
to look after me,
and you got me
to look after
you....
We got each other,
that's what,
that gives
a hoot in hell
about us....*

JOHN STEINBECK

*To your
good health,
old friend,
may you live
for a
thousand years,
and I be there
to count them.*

ROBERT SMITH SURTEES